LIFTOFF! SPACE EXPLORATION

REACHING THE MOON

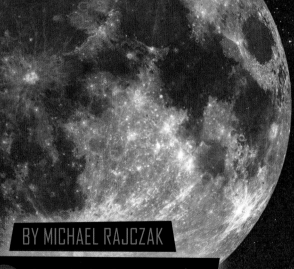

BY MICHAEL RAJCZAK

 Gareth Stevens
PUBLISHING

Please visit our website, www.garethstevens.com. For a free color catalog of all our high-quality books, call toll free 1-800-542-2595 or fax 1-877-542-2596.

Cataloging-in-Publication Data

Names: Rajczak, Michael.
Title: Reaching the moon / Michael Rajczak.
Description: New York : Gareth Stevens Publishing, 2021. | Series: Liftoff! space exploration | Includes glossary and index.
Identifiers: ISBN 9781538258743 (pbk.) | ISBN 9781538258767 (library bound) | ISBN 9781538258750 (6 pack)
Subjects: LCSH: Space flight to the moon–Juvenile literature. | Moon–Exploration–Juvenile literature.
Classification: LCC TL799.M6 R35 2021 | DDC 629.45'4–dc23

First Edition

Published in 2021 by
Gareth Stevens Publishing
111 East 14th Street, Suite 349
New York, NY 10003

Designer: Katelyn E. Reynolds
Editor: Abby Badach Doyle

Photo credits: Cover, p. 1 Vadim Sadovski/Shutterstock.com; cover, pp. 1–32 (series background) David M. Schrader/Shutterstock.com; p. 5 Castleski/Shutterstock.com; p. 7 SSPL/Getty Images; p. 9 (main) Sovfoto/Universal Images Group via Getty Images; p. 9 (inset) Bob Gomel/The LIFE Images Collection via Getty Images/Getty Images; p. 11 (main) NASA / Handout/Hulton Archive/Getty Images; pp. 11 (inset), 13 (main), 19 NASA; p. 13 (inset), 28 (Earth, Alan Shepard), 29 (moon, Neil Armstrong, *Apollo 17*) NASA/Space Frontiers/Getty Images; p. 15 (main) VCG Wilson/Corbis via Getty Images; p. 15 (inset) KSC/NASA; p. 17 (main) NASA/ullstein bild via Getty Images; p. 17 (inset) Lee Balterman/The LIFE Picture Collection via Getty Images; p. 21 © Corbis/Corbis via Getty Images; p. 23 NASA/Tom Tschida; p. 25 (main) Stocktrek Images/Getty Images; p. 25 (inset) Robert Markowitz - NASA - JSC; p. 27 NASA/Joel Kowsky; p. 29 (SpaceX) NASA/Tony Gray; Tim Powers; Tim Terry.

Printed in the United States of America

Some of the images in this book illustrate individuals who are models. The depictions do not imply actual situations or events.

CPSIA compliance information: Batch #CS20GS: For further information contact Gareth Stevens, New York, New York at 1-800-542-2595.

Find us on

CONTENTS

WORDS IN THE GLOSSARY APPEAR IN **BOLD** TYPE
THE FIRST TIME THEY ARE USED IN THE TEXT.

MYSTERIES OF THE MOON

It's likely people have been **fascinated** with the moon from the time the first humans looked up at it in the night sky. Still, the moon was a mystery for most of history. Artists have drawn and painted it. People have written songs about it. Ancient Greeks worshipped goddesses of the moon, such as Selene and Artemis.

Throughout history, people made up stories about the moon. In the Middle Ages, someone wondered if the moon was made of cheese! Some thought that there was a man's face on the moon.

Then, scientific thinkers began to make observations about the moon. Galileo Galilei used his early telescope to note that the moon was not smooth but had craters and mountains. Over time, a big question arose: Could people ever get to the moon?

INTERSTELLAR INFORMATION

THE MOON'S SURFACE IS MAINLY CHUNKS OF ROCK AND LIGHT GRAY DUST. IT HAS LONG DEAD VOLCANOES AND VERY OLD HARDENED LAVA FLOWS. THERE ARE MANY CRATERS FROM **ASTEROIDS** THAT HAVE LANDED THERE.

THE MOON'S PHASES

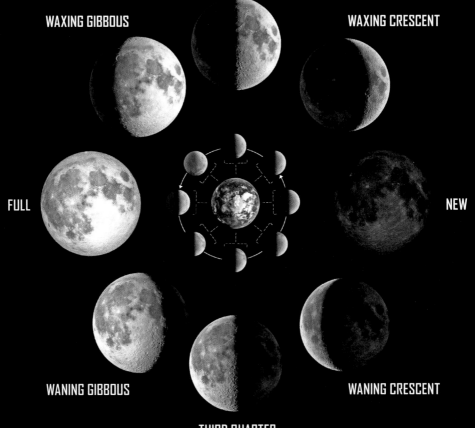

FIRST QUARTER

WAXING GIBBOUS

WAXING CRESCENT

FULL

NEW

WANING GIBBOUS

WANING CRESCENT

THIRD QUARTER

THE MOON SEEMS TO CHANGE ITS SHAPE EVERY DAY. IT
SEEMS NATURAL PEOPLE WOULD BE CURIOUS ABOUT IT!

HOW DID THE MOON FORM?

Scientists believe that the moon was formed about 4.5 billion years ago. One likely
theory, or idea, is that a very large object the size of a small planet collided with Earth.
This created a great amount of debris, such as many large pieces of rock. Some of
this was very hot. As it rotated around, enough gravity was created to pull these
many large pieces together. Over millions of years, it formed our round moon.

THE FIRST ROCKETS

The first rockets were made in China around 1232. They were gunpowder-filled tubes for weapons or fireworks. In the 1700s and 1800s, Europeans began to use rockets as weapons. Then, in 1889, Russian schoolteacher Konstantin Tsiolkovsky came up with the idea of using a rocket to get to space.

In the early 1900s, American Robert H. Goddard began building and launching rockets. In 1920, he proposed the possibility of a rocket to the moon. Instead of a solid fuel such as gunpowder, Goddard used liquid fuel. This made rockets more powerful. In Germany, Hermann Oberth promoted placing a small rocket on a larger rocket. It would use up the fuel in one stage. Then, a second stage would light to take the larger rocket higher and farther.

INTERSTELLAR INFORMATION

FORMER **NAZI** SCIENTIST WERNHER VON BRAUN WOULD CREATE MANY OF THE AMERICAN MISSILES AND ROCKETS. HE DESIGNED THE SATURN V ROCKET THAT CARRIED THE FIRST HUMANS TO THE MOON ON *APOLLO II*.

GERMAN ROCKETS

German scientists working with Oberth's rockets created the V-2, considered the first large rocket. This was a liquid fuel rocket used to launch bombs during World War II (1939–1945). Though it was not very successful in warfare, it became the starting point for both the rocket programs of the United States and the former Union of Soviet Socialist Republics (USSR). After World War II, 88 German rocket scientists came to the United States. Others went to the USSR.

THE SPACE RACE

After being **allies** during World War II, the United States and the USSR became rivals. The United States was angry about the Soviet takeover of Eastern Europe. The USSR didn't like that America seemed to be acting as the policeman of the world. The United States had developed an atomic bomb, so the USSR began developing one of its own. Both sides had brilliant scientists, including those from Germany, working to create rockets and missiles.

Each was trying to be the strongest military power. They competed around the world for influence and economic **domination**. The rivalry was known as the Cold War. It was not fought with armies. It was fought with spies and money. Each side wanted to prove that it was the biggest, best, and strongest.

INTERSTELLAR INFORMATION

IN MAY 1961, U.S. PRESIDENT JOHN F. KENNEDY LAID OUT A CHALLENGE TO SEND AN AMERICAN TO THE MOON AND BACK. IT BECAME A MATTER OF NATIONAL PRIDE TO BEAT THE SOVIETS TO THE MOON.

JOHN F. KENNEDY ▶

A BATTLE FOR FIRST

Early on, it seemed as though the United States was losing the Space Race, which is what people called the competition between the two countries to dominate in space. The USSR launched the first satellite and put the first man in space. Part of both the Cold War and the Space Race had to do with national safety. Satellites could be used to spy on your enemy. Some Americans became concerned that the Soviets would put weapons in space.

PROJECT MERCURY

Begun in 1958, Project Mercury's goals were simple. First, choose a safe and reliable rocket that could reach Earth's orbit. Military missiles served as guides. After trial and error and several explosions, the National **Aeronautics** and Space Administration (NASA) was able to make a safe rocket. The second goal was to put a person into orbit. NASA didn't know for sure that a human could survive liftoff and splashdown, or the landing of a spacecraft in the ocean. Three missions used a monkey and two chimpanzees before human flights were determined to be relatively safe.

Six of the flights were manned. The first two reached space and came right back down. Four of the flights orbited Earth. Some thought of the astronauts as just passengers on a satellite, but the astronauts saw themselves as pilots of their spacecrafts.

INTERSTELLAR INFORMATION

ABOUT 62 MILES (100 KM) AWAY FROM EARTH IS GENERALLY ACCEPTED AS THE BOUNDARY BETWEEN AIR SPACE AND OUTER SPACE. ALTHOUGH MOST SCIENTISTS HAVE AGREED UPON THIS, IT'S NOT CONSIDERED AN EXACT FIXED DISTANCE.

HAM THE CHIMPANZEE PREPARES FOR HIS MERCURY FLIGHT. ▶

THE FIRST AMERICANS IN SPACE

Alan Shephard was a Project Mercury astronaut and the first American to reach space. On May 5, 1961, Shephard's spacecraft *Freedom 7* traveled a total of 300 miles (482 km). His trip lasted about 15 minutes. On February 20, 1962, John Glenn became the first American to orbit Earth. While he orbited, there was a problem with some equipment that put a safe reentry into Earth's atmosphere in question. Glenn used his skill as a pilot to have a safe splashdown.

11

GEMINI
PAVES THE WAY

The next step on the road to the moon was the Gemini program. Of the 19 missions, 10 of them carried two astronauts at a time. The Gemini flights had a set of goals to build on the knowledge and experiences gained in the Mercury program. One goal was to stay in space as long as a mission would take to the moon. Another was to perfect the spacecraft **maneuvers** needed to go from Earth's orbit toward the moon and back. This included practicing changing orbits.

The astronauts practiced docking, or linking up safely with another spacecraft. These other spacecraft were launched separately, and it was the job of the astronauts to locate and link up with them. Gemini missions also helped NASA improve reentry into Earth's atmosphere and the safety of the splashdown.

INTERSTELLAR INFORMATION

THE GEMINI MISSIONS WERE THE FIRST TO USE NASA'S NEW MISSION CONTROL CENTER IN HOUSTON, TEXAS. WHILE THE ASTRONAUTS WERE LEARNING HOW TO MANEUVER IN SPACE, THE CREW ON THE GROUND WAS WORKING DAILY TO IMPROVE THEIR SUPPORTING ROLES.

◀ *GEMINI 5* SPLASHDOWN, 1965

SPACEWALKS

Gemini missions had astronauts work outside of the spacecraft. These were known as
spacewalks. The NASA term for this is extravehicular activity, or EVA. Ed White was the first
American to walk in space. He used a hand-held device that shot out small puffs
of air that helped him move. The astronauts discovered that they needed hand railings,
footholds, and a tether to safely move outside of the spacecraft.

13

APOLLO
REACHES THE MOON

The Apollo program eventually launched 11 successful manned missions. However, there was trouble at the beginning. On January 27, 1967, NASA was testing the first command **module** on the launch pad when a fire broke out. All three astronauts on board died. Because of this, NASA decided to test equipment in some unmanned missions before moving forward.

In October 1968, *Apollo 7* became the first mission with three astronauts. They practiced separating and docking the command and service modules while orbiting Earth. It was necessary to practice, since this would need to happen in the moon's orbit. *Apollo 8* was the first manned spacecraft to orbit the moon. *Apollo 9* also orbited the moon. *Apollo 10*'s crew practiced everything for a moon landing. These missions showed that the United States was ready to land astronauts on the moon.

INTERSTELLAR INFORMATION

WHILE ON THE FAR SIDE OF THE MOON, ASTRONAUTS LOSE CONTACT WITH NASA'S MISSION CONTROL. THE REASON IS THAT WHEN THE MOON IS IN BETWEEN THE ASTRONAUTS AND EARTH, IT BLOCKS ALL RADIO COMMUNICATIONS.

◀ INSIDE THE LUNAR MODULE, *APOLLO 11*

MAIN PARTS

A complete Apollo spacecraft featured three parts. The service module contained the engine. The command module was the cone-shaped capsule where astronauts worked and slept. This part brought the astronauts back through Earth's atmosphere too. Parachutes in the nose would come out, slowing the capsule down for a safe splashdown in the ocean. The third part was the lunar module. This was the vehicle used by two of the astronauts for landing on the moon.

THE EAGLE HAS LANDED

"That's one small step for a man; one giant leap for mankind." With those words, Neil Armstrong stepped off of the *Apollo 11* lunar module, nicknamed the Eagle, and became the first human to set foot on the moon. Twenty minutes later, Edwin "Buzz" Aldrin became the second. The third crew member, Michael Collins, remained in orbit in the command module. All three had been astronauts in the Gemini program too.

The astronauts planted an American flag and laid down objects to honor Americans and Russians who had died trying to get to the moon. Armstrong and Aldrin collected over 47 pounds (21.3 kg) of rock and soil. Armstrong spent 2.5 hours exploring the surface, traveling about 3,300 feet (1 km). He and Aldrin spent 21.5 hours on the moon before they began their trip to return home to Earth.

INTERSTELLAR INFORMATION

APOLLO 13 WAS SUPPOSED TO BRING THE THIRD GROUP OF AMERICAN ASTRONAUTS TO THE MOON. AFTER AN OXYGEN TANK EXPLOSION, THE CREW USED SEVERAL EMERGENCY PROCEDURES JUST TO BE ABLE TO MAKE IT HOME SAFELY.

MORE THAN 600 MILLION PEOPLE TUNED IN TO LIVE TELEVISION TO WATCH NEIL ARMSTRONG AND BUZZ ALDRIN WALK ON THE MOON.

FIVE MORE MOON LANDINGS

Six more missions to the moon were planned, but only five made it. Those missions were numbered *Apollo 12, 14, 15, 16,* and *17.* Each mission collected rock and soil samples and took photos. Scientific equipment was left behind to monitor **seismic** activity. Astronauts even rode in a moon buggy! NASA was able to learn a great deal about the conditions on the moon. The missions showed how humans could work and survive on the moon.

LEAVING THE MOON

With each mission, astronauts stayed longer and explored farther. However, no matter how many rocks they collected or how much scientists learned, many Americans thought the Apollo program was a waste of money and resources. In fact, most public opinion polls throughout the 1960s and 1970s showed that about half of Americans thought the government was spending too much money on space.

It takes billions of dollars and many engineers and scientists to run a space program. In the 1970s, some people thought those resources should be taking care of other problems, such as hunger or education. Over time, NASA received less money. The space agency had to put aside some projects and focus on new goals. One was the International Space Station (ISS). Another was the space shuttle program.

INTERSTELLAR INFORMATION

PRESIDENT RICHARD NIXON CANCELED WHAT WOULD HAVE BEEN *APOLLO 18, 19,* AND *20.* THIS WAS DONE TO SAVE MONEY IN THE GOVERNMENT'S BUDGET.

WHAT ELSE WE LEARNED FROM THE MOON

The Apollo program expanded our knowledge not only about the moon, but also about Earth. During Projects Mercury, Gemini, and Apollo, the most advanced cameras ever created up to that time took thousands of pictures of Earth from space. Astronauts discovered that the moon has a smell, like spent fireworks. Inventions such as solar panels, advanced fabrics used by firefighters, and cordless tools are based on Apollo technologies. Others include internal heart monitors and shock-absorbing sneakers!

19

SPACE STATIONS

With six successful U.S. trips to land astronauts on the moon, the question became: What's next? Some thought that we should make a base on the moon. Others were focused on going to Mars. This was a time when the United States and the USSR (modern-day Russia) were enjoying a period of better cooperation.

While the U.S. was going to the moon, the USSR was putting the first space station into orbit. The USSR put seven Salyut space stations into orbit starting in 1971. It placed the first module of the Mir space station into orbit in 1986. The United States launched its space station, called Skylab, in 1973 using leftover pieces from the Apollo program. All of these stations were difficult to maintain. Eventually, each was allowed to burn up in Earth's atmosphere.

INTERSTELLAR INFORMATION

THE ISS HAS BEEN REGULARLY OCCUPIED SINCE NOVEMBER 2, 2000.

REUSING PIECES FROM THE APOLLO PROGRAM TO CREATE SKYLAB HELPED NASA SAVE MONEY DURING A TIME WHEN ITS BUDGET WAS BEING CUT.

THE INTERNATIONAL SPACE STATION

People from 19 countries (and counting!) have visited the ISS. Its main partners are NASA, Russia, the European Space Agency (ESA), Japan, and Canada. By having such cooperation, the cost of building and maintaining the space station is not the responsibility of just one country. Operating a successful space station may help engineers and scientists learn how to build a successful base on the moon. The ISS will play an important role in future moon missions.

21

SPACE SHUTTLES

Imagine a vehicle that launches like a rocket and lands like an airplane. That is exactly what the space shuttles did for 30 years. From 1981 until 2011, five space shuttles flew a total of 135 flights. The shuttle could place satellites in orbit, capture satellites for repair, and haul cargo to space stations. Space shuttles carried pieces of the ISS into orbit. It could carry up to eight astronauts at a time.

A reusable space plane was considered a key part of future moon missions and a mission to Mars. Some say the shuttles were like moving vans. A space shuttle delivered the Hubble Space Telescope to Earth's orbit. The technology that went into the space shuttles will help advance future spacecraft that will take humans back to the moon.

INTERSTELLAR INFORMATION

TWO SPACE SHUTTLE MISSIONS ENDED IN DISASTER. *CHALLENGER* EXPLODED SHORTLY AFTER LIFTOFF IN 1986, AND *COLUMBIA* BURNED UP UPON REENTRY THROUGH EARTH'S ATMOSPHERE IN 2003. BETWEEN THE TWO ACCIDENTS, 14 ASTRONAUTS LOST THEIR LIVES.

A TOTAL OF 355 INDIVIDUAL PEOPLE FLEW ON NASA'S FIVE SPACE SHUTTLES: *COLUMBIA, CHALLENGER, DISCOVERY, ATLANTIS,* AND *ENDEAVOUR.*

ATLANTIS

BY THE NUMBERS

The space shuttles orbited Earth at the speed of 17,500 miles (27,359 km) per hour. That means that you can see a sunrise every 90 minutes. In their 30-year history, the space shuttles' combined number of miles traveled is over half a billion (more than 8 billion km). John Glenn, a former Mercury astronaut, was the oldest shuttle astronaut at age 77. Glenn returned to space in October 1998 aboard the space shuttle *Discovery.*

OTHER NATIONS' MOON MISSIONS

Through the years, the United States wasn't the only country trying to explore the moon. In 1959, the USSR's Luna 2 was the first spacecraft to land on the moon, but it crashed. In 1966, the Luna 9 made a soft landing and took the first close-up pictures. The Soviets sent rovers to the moon, but never a person.

The beginnings of the China National Space Program started in the 1950s. It focused mostly on rocket development. Its first manned mission was in 2003, when Yang Liwei flew a 21-hour solo mission. In December 2013, China landed an unmanned **probe** with a moon rover. Today, China continues to have the most success with moon missions. In 2019, the Chang'e 4 probe sent a rover to explore the far side of the moon.

INTERSTELLAR INFORMATION

JAXA IS JAPAN'S SPACE AGENCY. IT HAS SENT PROBES TO VENUS AND THE SUN. ITS FIRST ASTRONAUT WAS MAMORU MOHRI WHO FLEW ABOARD NASA'S SPACE SHUTTLE *ENDEAVOUR* IN 1992.

THE CANADIAN SPACE AGENCY, WHICH STARTED
IN 1989, DEVELOPS ROBOTS AND HAS SENT
ASTRONAUTS SUCH AS JULIE PAYETTE TO THE ISS.

A TEAM EFFORT IN EUROPE

The ESA was created in 1975. It includes membership from 22 European nations. By combining the resources of many nations, it can do much more than any single European nation could achieve. One of ESA's greatest contributions to human spaceflight is helping to build and run the ISS. The ESA sends astronauts to the space station. Additionally, the ESA launches satellites, and in 2003 placed its Mars Express satellite around Mars.

GOING BACK SOON

Many people think that the next astronaut on the moon will be Chinese. China has announced plans to send astronauts to the moon's southern pole and establish a research station there. After hearing about China's **ambitious** lunar program, NASA set a goal of returning to the moon by 2024. This time, some parts of the space program have been **contracted** to private companies.

Two of those companies are SpaceX and Blue Origin. SpaceX's Dragon spacecraft already delivers cargo to the International Space Station. Soon, it may carry astronauts there. SpaceX has said it wants to take people to the moon and even Mars. Blue Origin has also carried cargo to the ISS. NASA has chosen Blue Origin to develop the next lunar landing craft.

INTERSTELLAR INFORMATION

INDIA ATTEMPTED TO LAND A PROBE ON THE MOON IN 2019, BUT IT CRASHED. ISRAEL ALSO IS ATTEMPTING TO LAND A LUNAR PROBE.

THE NEXT GENERATION OF ASTRONAUTS IN THE ARTEMIS PROGRAM WILL HAVE NEW SPACESUITS WITH BETTER TECHNOLOGY AND SAFETY EQUIPMENT.

THE ARTEMIS PROGRAM

In Greek mythology, Artemis is Apollo's twin sister and goddess of the Moon. NASA's Artemis program plans to land the first woman and the next man on the moon. The rockets, robotics, and other technologies are being developed by companies hoping to make money. They are charging NASA a fee for the work they provide. They may also allow private citizens to pay to go into space. There is even talk of mining the moon for rare minerals.

In 1962, President John F. Kennedy gave a now-famous speech. In it, he set an ambitious goal for the United States to get a man to the moon and back in less than 10 years. He spoke about the importance of making space a place for peace and science.

Today, NASA is planning the Gateway, a smaller space station which will orbit the moon and serve as a sort of home base there. The first piece is set to be launched in 2022. After that, the world has it eyes on Mars. Today, the 34-million mile (54.7-million km) trip seems like a difficult goal. However, as you are reading this, there are thousands of people hard at work to make that dream a reality in your lifetime!

TIMELINE
TO THE MOON AND BACK

FEBRUARY 20, 1962
JOHN GLENN BECOMES THE FIRST MAN TO ORBIT EARTH.

APRIL 12, 1961
YURI GAGARIN OF THE USSR BECOMES THE FIRST MAN IN SPACE.

MAY 5, 1961
ALAN SHEPARD BECOMES THE FIRST AMERICAN IN SPACE.

MAY 23, 2019
NASA ANNOUNCES ARTEMIS PROGRAM TIMETABLE TO RETURN TO THE MOON IN 2024.

DECEMBER 11, 2017
PRESIDENT TRUMP SIGNS SPACE POLICY DIRECTIVE 1 THAT INCLUDES A U.S. RETURN TO THE MOON.

DECEMBER 8, 2010
SPACEX SUCCESSFULLY LAUNCHES ITS DRAGON CAPSULE INTO EARTH'S ORBIT, BECOMING THE FIRST PRIVATE COMPANY TO DO SO.

NOVEMBER 20, 1998
THE FIRST PIECE OF THE INTERNATIONAL SPACE STATION IS PLACED IN ORBIT.

APRIL 12, 1981
THE FIRST SPACE SHUTTLE, *COLUMBIA*, IS LAUNCHED.

DECEMBER 19, 1972
THE LAST U.S. MANNED MOON MISSION *APOLLO 17* RETURNS TO EARTH.

JULY 20, 1969
NEIL ARMSTRONG BECOMES THE FIRST MAN ON THE MOON.

MARCH 23, 1965
THE FIRST MANNED GEMINI MISSION LAUNCHES WITH TWO ASTRONAUTS ON BOARD.

GLOSSARY

aeronautics: a science that deals with airplanes and flying

allies: countries who work together toward a goal

ambitious: having a strong desire to succeed

asteroid: a large rock or small planet-like object that circles the sun

contract: a formal agreement or business deal

domination: control or power over something

fascinate: to command interest or attention strongly

maneuver: planned movement that requires skill

module: an independently operable unit that is part of a spacecraft

Nazi: a member of a German political party that controlled Germany from 1933 to 1945 under Adolf Hitler

probe: an unmanned spacecraft that travels through space to collect science information

satellite: an object that circles Earth in order to collect and send information or aid in communication

seismic: having to do with an earthquake or movement of a planet's crust

FOR MORE INFORMATION

BOOKS

Abbott, Simon. *100 Questions About Outer Space*. White Plains, NY: Peter Pauper Press, 2018

Pohlen, Jerome. *The Apollo Missions for Kids: The People and Engineering Behind the Race to the Moon, with 21 Activities*. Chicago, IL: Chicago Review Press, 2019.

Woolf, Alex. *Trailblazers: Neil Armstrong*. London, United Kingdom: Stripes Publishing, 2019.

WEBSITES

All About the Moon
spaceplace.nasa.gov/all-about-the-moon/en/
Learn about the moon with pictures and real photos from space on this NASA website just for kids.

Learning from What Apollo Astronauts Left on the Moon
www.sciencenewsforstudents.org/article/learning-what-apollo-astronauts-left-moon
Fun facts and interesting maps explain what humans left behind during moon missions.

The Moon Landing
kids.nationalgeographic.com/explore/history/moon-landing/
Read about the Space Race and the *Apollo 11* mission that landed the first humans on the moon.

INDEX